A PSALMISTRY

BY THE

NEW
KING DAVID

YAARON WILLIAMS

authorHOUSE®

AuthorHouse™
1663 Liberty Drive
Bloomington, IN 47403
www.authorhouse.com
Phone: 1 (800) 839-8640

Published by AuthorHouse   04/05/2017

ISBN: 978-1-5246-8718-2 (sc)
ISBN: 978-1-5246-8717-5 (e)

Print information available on the last page.

INTRODUCTION

Books have been written for and of your every thought in mind and for many reasons. They entice the world and pull at your beliefs. Words of material things, love, money, death and of every season. Books of many types, written by both men and women. Letters to you from all parts. The one that I love tho has my best interest at heart. So read these words straight from the hips. A highlight of reminder is, that they are like eating a sandwhich as you fight for more potatoe chips.

Birds who are they? they come and they go. So many different ones of all stripes. They seem to appear whether it rains or it snows. Some harmless such as doves. Some so regal such as eagals. But to me all are majestic in there own way. You never know when they might appear, whether at night or at day. Catch them if you can, but they may slip from your hands. Wise are they to do their duty. And they seem to do it without impunity. They have been around since the beginning of time. I have even thought of being as such, but then I thought to myself, wait a minute they don't wine. Oh what a creation GOD made. As they sing and dance for HIM returning the favor. They even seem to praise HIM. I wonder sometimes. How much did I do today.

2

Do not wait for me, for you are not strong, Do not wait for me, for you are not of my kind, Do not wait for me, for you are not mine. Do not wait for me, for I do not know of you. Do not wait for me, for you have no gold. But wait! there is one who should never say this to you, A MOM. And ONE WHO WILL NEVER SAY THIS TO YOU. JESUS, The SON of GOD.

3

Why did I go to her? Why did I let her woo me in with her curious seductions?, when her looks were not even so tantilizing nor sparkling nor bubbly. But now snared like a bird for a meal. I plead to be set free of her grasp. And now I hear the obvious voidness of her replies and laugh, as if to say. But where will you go? since you have left your faith. So then stay with me and learn to have doupt, and enjoy the many reductions.

4

Can you see me? Can you hold me? Can you teach me? Can you feed me? Can you keep me? Can you wipe my tears away? Can you kiss me? Can you forgive me? Can you give me strength when I am weak? Can I live with you like I am filthy? As I was sitting alone one day. A scroll of questions marched my way. So my heart intervened as if to say. Why do you feel guilty? For of today, because I want to be a good angel. I make no haste, as to bother my soul concerning of what good deed that I must do for those who are of famiar faces, whether or not they may do the same. What must matter of the utmost is that my true honor be sustained.

I heard a glass vase say to me one day. Why did you put those flowers in me? I cleaned my glass door window pane and heard it say to me, why are you getting me wet? I rolled down my glass windsheild on my car and heard it say, why can' t you keep me still sometimes? My perscription glassess do not seem to work as they should any more. Which left me to pray to GOD. Help me to be obediante, also to know why I was made. Because YOU are The MAKER of this fragile glass. And just that (YOU) have touch me. Makes me very glad.

Love who made thee? Love, why have you skipped over me? Love I have been asking for thee. Love, why have you have cracked my heart in to many places? when all I wanted was to sit by thee and grow my wings. Why? love, why? Her reply was, Who are you to me? and did you not know that I am void without directions from above. And their is where you should redirect your questions. And HE WHOM is their, you should call upon by name, HE has power over me and HIS HAND I fit in like a glove.

Hidden in waiting is an answer, but she is hard to reconcile with, because she can imtimidate all situations and block all entry ways. Her price cannot be negotiated if she chooses her stay. She can strike the king of men to his knees to ask for a compromise of moments and times of the future, as well as that of the past. She can come to a stop or crawl as a snale to make one beg. But when she gives up or delivers the most. Her praise is screamed out and honored any way. Even more than the smell of wonderful flowers on a spring day. As her nectar is fully delivered, it can be absorbed and digested as she is fully emptied out. Yet still, even as time moves around her, and though she commands much respect. She to must reverence JEHOVAH, THE LORD of HOST.

8

A sweet moment, A sweet kiss, A sweet thing, A sweet thought, A sweet day, The smell of a sweet flower, A sweet gesture from a person. Of all these I may desire or wish. And yet none can compare to SWEET JESUS.

I ponderd the reason of seasons. Since everything seems to have season. So then, I did as tought and went to wisdom to ask it of seasons. Wisdom seem to take me to missions. Since all things do have a season, I began to hear of wisdom, as it said. To complete a mission for a reason. You may not always understand the reason, but the mission for any season will be complete; so then this is what you must grow to understand.

10

Stop dreaming and you may awaken. Stop breathing and you will truley live, because the sun goes down it does not end the days. Because the moon is sheilded by the storm does not mean that there is no hope the next day. When a goodbye is said, a hello is raised. An ant lives after the flood and then goes across any stone. So then should my feet crush any turmoil to make the lifespan of true love to be always and everlasting.

11

A wheel was made to roll and still does. A promise made by man should be kept. A stone is carved without a previous blueprint. A dance can be created for many to repeat, and a host problems are solved on the earth. But who can say where 'GOD' lives.

12

There they are aloft in the sky, clouds; for they are so beatiful floating past one's eyes. Without wings, without a care in the world. No hands or strings to hold them up. Nor that move them north, south, east, or west. Oceans in the sky. Promises made and promises kepted. Waters in discret. Life not thought of at times. Workers of "THE ALMIGHTY". They are team members with the other elements to help sustain life on earth for "HIM." There they are, doing a work like kisses on a body. Oh! the dreams that they fulfill. And the exspectations also are equivelent. As they dance floating by, surpassing the glory of the moon at night. And even the sun at daylight. Oh what a mystery concerning them. What task do they have next? ONLY! GOD ALMIGHTY knows. Because I have not figuried them out as of yet. So let there floating keep ging.

13

Up above in a secret place, a stone came down and hit me in face. It broke no bones nor torn any flesh. And had the tast of clean fresh air. With that touch my speech and limbs were unbound to dare. Yet from that place, whence gave to me such wonderful grace. Yet still no man can live at that location. But blessed Im I now to say. That HE only and HIS allowed hosts, can dewell in outer space. All they have are thoughts of pure actions. And below There feet, die every foul mistake and provocation.

Who's fields, have I wonderd into? Some are so plentiful with a variaty of plants and trees, of many shapes and colors, even on every border. It can be so easy to get full in it. So many places to turn to in it, so many directions to get lost because of it. If I turn left or right their is a place to eat from it, the same is true as with up or down, meaning the great skys and the great seas, which both seems to breath. They all seem to be none void because there was a way that they could be replenished, so the volume of them never really does deminish. But who did it? So I ask on this journey. I feel asleep one night to catch the stars to ask of them, how do you feed?, As I mentioned the beauti of there endless fields. They did not reply to me, and only continued looking in the same direction and singing praises as to show me (HE) that feeds them, and keeps all so equal.

15

I am beautiful. Iam beautiful because YOU are here, I am beautiful because YOU are near, I am beautiful because YOU are strong, I am beautiful even when I blunder, I am beautiful because YOU are my friend, I am beautiful because YOU saved me, I am beautiful because YOU cover my weaknessess, I am beautiful because YOU make a way for me. YOUR looks reflect my desire and hunger. So Thank YOU LORD for placing my beauti in all of YOUR WONDER.

16

When I fly with YOU, oh I just can't wait. When I fly with YOU it will be a great day. When I fly with YOU, I shall surpass the birds. When I fly with YOU, my tears will melt away. When I fly with YOU, I will lose the hurt. When I fly away with YOU holding my hand. I will be totaly free, because I am now with YOU where I should be. But as I fly with YOU I will remember to reach out to my fellow man, because when YOU made me, YOU gave me two hands.

Royalty or Majesty, Which one might I choose? I go where they seem to exsist, to the Eagle and the stallion, in the open field. The eagle goes low and high at will, with no interruptions, at any speed, and marking all angles and points with commanding grace by the wings. The stallion, born to be a prince of the praire commanding much respect by lighting type speed, with the sound like that of thunder from there feet. With hair like that of silver plates glistening from the suns beem. And he knows all of mares are looking because they stare. So which is the pick?. There is no debate! I will just keep humility for now since it helps me to live and keeps me in my place.

18

Oh, LORD who is she that makes me cry? I dream of her often that is why. I see her in the nights and look for her in the day. But when I look in there eyes they look away. Why do I desire of her?, when she will only try to led me astray. I have tried to rebuke her, but she follows me all day. I think that I need her to calm my ways. It is her love that I think that I want at times. But from what I've learned it can never be mine. Her beauti has seduced me that is why I whine. And such would not have happened if I had only kepted my place in line. So please help to renew my strength again as a man of YOUR DIVINE.

19

Who works all night and plays all day?. Only a fool who does not know of his stay. Doesen't he know of rest for a day. No one will exzault you in the grave. Misguided like a castaway, I swam across the ocean to catch a meal, only to see that it was swimming with me, the whole time, the whole way. It kepted me from drowning and becoming a meal. And now without my lost desires. I finially awakend, turned around and made it back to the beach and fell alseep alive safe and sound.

20

No oceans are so deep as words.
No stare so far as the milkyways.
No heart so big as to stop love.
No days so long as to stop a right.
No pain so incurable as to stop the cure, No amount of riches can remove the stain of death, No style can cover a lie, No flood can destroy a true measure, And no movement is done without a thought first made. But, still the wind blows, the trees still move. So then such is the Existence of the Presence of GOD.

21

In YOU oh LORD is where I dance. In YOU oh LORD IS where I make my stand, because the days with YOU are never boring, joy, life, hope has been the story. What could be next in this adventer? who knows? because YOU have no book ends.

22

Trails and bridges are ment to cross. Lies and love maybe the same. Bet on either when there is no route, and you may lose a fortune all in one life time.

23

Overcast was there forecast all day. But why did not anyone tell me that my love would of me say. I do not want you anymore it was all a mistake.

24

She whispered, I will love you till I die, as she kiss me, shed a tear, and layed her head on me till the sun rise. Then tomorrow at dawn she began to screamed. You mean nothing to me, depart from me, you scandrol, you nothing, you worthless thing. As I pleaded to her, oh my love, no; what have I DONE? Her simple reply was. Did you not know, the game and that this is what I do for fun.

Pain, why go to such levels? Wishing on a star, dreaming of forever romance, Put much in, to get so little out. Is this the moment that I am no longer lonely. Can I capture the essence of singing bird to solve my starving? Who wrote this script? Who brought such tease. I don't know. But without THE LORD, the pain would be much more severe.

26

Sing a song to the deaf; over pay a dept to many times; tell a whore that our love will be forever; make your way under the cloulds to wash the tears away. Is is not easyer to just say. Oh! what a fool am I, before for they do, making your sadness much more easer to tolerate.

27

I can control the pitch of love, I can control the rains. I can make the moon appear again tomorrow night, and control the ways of men. Men, why I have them eating out of my hands. But her heart had departed from him, as soon as he said to her. The doors have all closed, I am about to go to my maker. To contribe love by boastful words is not my way. For the ficalness of a heart can be swayed with very little payment. But in the end return such a low interest.

28

These words came to me, as I burst into laughter, as I was waiting for the birth of my son. But then my true peak hit. The matrurity of life that is to say. The way that things are, sadness, tears, joy, death, run. The emotions of the day. As my recordings began to play. what is reality? And the way that things must be. The answer was always within me. Child just Pray.

29

She replied, why should i keep my heart in check?, why should i keep my heart at bay?, only to recieve a wage of little pence as some slave would at the end of the day. But her grandmother replied with a smile. Child just as the dross must be removed from silver and before that even from the clay, or as the trees never stop growing because there leaves fell that day. So you must go through changes as well as times, and learn to wait.

30

Who can figure out a rhyme, but yet keep his rhythem in his climb, up a very high mountain without getting a bloody nose after reaching the top of the rise? Then swim the deepest of the oceans without becoming a meal. And may escape the wiles of a thousand woman in a life time, before they can catch his subtil appeal. But then makes it to the end of his road, only now to see that he still must give thanks, and pay his due toll. Just because we don't notice the price tag. Does not mean that it's not present, that is what I have been told.

31

Behold, the wind, it comes, it goes from where nobody seems to know. It comes from the north, or south, the east and the west. At spring it arrives so sweet. At winter with a blizzard. It screams and whispers. A hum a cry, it even sounds like it's singing. Day or night it may put you to bed. When it is still, that's weird, one may think that it is dead. But no not so fast. For just keep living, because here it is again, just like in the past, from whence I do not know. But it is a wonder to me, the same as fire, rain, and snow. just don't count it out as you breath, for as with that, I thank GOD for the next breeze.

32

You must come up to heaven at least once, if you are trying to find true love and it's worth. Did not any one tell you that you will not find it with your head in the sand and your face in the dirt. Oh no, come up here to see what you have been looking for. Then you will believe. The path to it is so wonderful and the way to it is so clear. You may think that you are going to slip and fall. But oh no! did you not read. Read before your jearney the best book of all. For it spoke of love in much detail. Love is GOD and JESUS, THEY are everywhere start where you are, believe.

33

Trees and love seem to have one thing in common. And that is they can be exchanged for any amount of money or dollar. The bargain is high, the bargain is low. Who ever is sure where either one will pop up or grow. Both seem as if to die suddenly for no reason, only to reappear at another season. Sometimes it's as if they have there own masters. As many watch them come and go in different disasters. I wonder of the two as I watch for where they might fall. Because when one of them does you may be left black and blue, no matter who you are.

34

I remember my childhood as much as I can, but no one told me that it could be done with chains on my hands. The chains of life which pull me foward towards my future destiny and the new chains that I must exspore. But are these really chains or just somethings that I should ignore. Breaking away from them seems a task, a chore. As I ponder there strenghts and whether they are locked or unlock, or if the keys are in my hands. A fathom, a mystery, a mind thing, lack of faith. I don't know. But I MUST FIGURE OUT HOW TO BREAK AWAY from every band.

35

A dream without hope is like honey and no bees. A walk in the night without knowing where you've been. No air, to blow on the trees. To hug, but not delivering the final kiss. Oh, what began this maze of bliss? I don't know because I was still aleep when I was walking through the forest and looking at the green.

36

Why ever lose your heart or the path to a belief. Don't! The sun keeps it's shine and moon it's gleen. Has not the cricket remain to make noise at the edge of the stream. For the life from it is more than can be seen. The darkness may come, yet the waters may flood. But if we stay high above them, we will even enhance our soar. Then we will fufill a mission as they have, without a notice.

37

On one particliar moment, just a particlar day, I watched as the birds all flew in group and turned to notice a family with kids at play. I thought to myself don't they know that this is only a malaze. A blip on a screen, as some early morning daze. With the fog in my heart, I said, I can't perticpate; no, no, not me; not in this race. But I met her one day at the end of the spring. Looked in her eyes, kissed her and soon gave her a ring. So now here I am doing what I thought was only in vain and now laugh at those thoughts from the past of which I should have learned to disdained.

38

Awake, awake I say after the night is broken at the will of the day, Awake all living because of it without delay. Arise to do it, as dew does on the bay, as the morning tender breeze also submits a notice proving the suns authority and it's array. For who reminds it to awaken at any second, or minute, any hour of the day. Before you or I had heard that word awake. The sun did listen to the command from HE that is above, to do it's work and awake, but all it needed was just one word from HIM. And that word was simply, Stay.

39

On this phatom plain I've been to the gate of the city's a storm, where there were vipers to try to prove me wrong, I arose made it to the oceans to have waves stand up high to delay my crossing, made it at my other destination of the mountains to find a surrounding fortress. But still I made it to the top to release my scream. Never did I touch the ground again until I reached heaven. Because I kepted my way. Yes I believed.

40

Say to yourself I have no hope. Is like saying to yourself I cannot eat. It is not neccesary to think on it, just let it flow like sand under your feet. And before you know. It will pull you in deep. Like a summer storm putting you to sleep. Just breath it in and out as easly as you can. And now look, just like that, you'all see that it's like breathing, You have hope in your hands. But don't forget to nurish that seed, so it will always give you sweet, sweet dreams.

41

Like sugar and spice, I beg to differ that girls are not sweet as candy as they say. Or not even ok because they marry some rich nice dude named randy. I say that they are of animal unique, Because of the ingrediates inwhich that they are made, making them more tasty than any other tasty treats. For me especially, the wholesome one's, which are all natrual and full of JESUS. Mixed and made by HIS HAND with grace, faith and humility. Just one bit into this one, and my mind would say, PLEASE, PLEASE. But then soon after I would have to repeat. THANK YOU LORD! for fufilling my every need. Because no chef on earth could have made her better than THEE.

I had heard that there is a thin line between love and hate. So I got sick of hearing it and pulled out my measuring tape. Let's see hate is stupid, hate is evil, hate is disgraceful and is a waste. So let's end this debate. Now to measure love. Love is good, love is strong, love is healthy and can help you to live long. Guess some (could not see) that they were that for apart. And the end of that thought is, stay out of the HATE FOG.

43

Was I so wrong, was I so green? Thinking of her, singing as I walked down the streets. In a daze every so often, even staring at the trees. My mind had not replaced the memories of such a pleasent thing. But that, I thought that I could handle. And when thoughts appeared to say, go by and see her, buy some flowers. Maybe it will rekindle, maybe it will last. But like a breeze, I rememered the past, and the words that she uttered. Please go away, leave me alone, because being around you reminds me of some bad song.

 **44**

I think of love, but it is so hard to figure out. Like science or math or some truckers road map. One day it's up, the next day it is down, just as some drama clown. But then I put it to a study, as with people to figure it out. So here is the final answer of the whole delima. Love is tall, love is wishy washy, love is fickle, love is short, love can be to heavy at times. And all because love needs a master. And the fact is, without GOD ALMIGHTY, just like with people who don't chose HIM. Love becomes a disaster.

45

I run to YOU, my GOD, because their is no where else to run. Thrown away sometimes like a castaway, and many times under the gun. I fish for YOUR EMBRACE like a flower does seeeking for the warmth and light of the sun. And after my plea for HIS REST; I am sure that I will be ok. Because their is no harm or emptyness at HIS LOCATION. There are no snake bits or barks of the dogs at HIS PLACE. And in HIM one get's full and healthy, because HIS SON, HIS LIGHT, feds me all day. But even if they did not turn, or betray, at times at my presence, it is still better this way. For a child should know there PARENT, (YOU), and where YOU stay.

46

I would not dance at there parade, I did not sing to receive there release of hate. I also stared at there food at there dinner table. There smiles of contempt I veried from, even at noonday. Even there partys were to lose with tainted games of play. As they snubbed there noses as I prayed. I remembered soon afterwards, very quickly, Who gave to me my blessings. And that thought I shall keep. Because it is my life's staple.

47

By stars and rain drops many have made there wishes. It is funny, that because of fire and water we can even wash our dishies. The both may decend when people least expect. They both are above human heads. They capture the hearts of men when it is depressed. I guess we should say that they help to equilize our moments of mess. Or they help to remove a time of doupt, to make a little time of hope seed. To take one out from a dark clould. It's not just by chance when this occurs. But formulated by Love, that is to say. Done by THE LORD, SIGN HE, LOVE UP ABOVE.

48

Keep your stones don't throw them at me, for they will only miss to go into the abyss. You aim them in a direction from your hollow place. Laugh as you try for a hit in any location. Attempt high or low, as to make some brake. As a young bull before his time seeking his mate. I to can laugh because I have an esscape. And I know of how the wicked usaully operate. For it is always the same, very easy to say, here they are again blinded by there own bloody drink.

49

Answers, answers who really has them? I 've got some here wait and see. Oh, I just forgot what I was sopose to say, because I was not listening in the past to what the wise one's had to say. They had a lot of words with answers like bricks made to build a house. But in some way they seemed back then, as little as a mouse. Not so now, as I scramble to find them in my minds lost and found. Better do it quick, before the next conversation. For who needs someone that does a lot of thought blinking. When what is needed are words that will help, and are always sound.

50

The wages of time are in the turn. In the cycle of the wheel thrown by the motion of the process, a choice has been born. An equal balance, a leveled sheet. No different than the ways of the universe. Though alive in the darkness. The life is in the parts of your moving wheel. A lot is cast by the spinning. Just as there is no way to get the diamonds unless there is some digging. As a hand must decide to go deep in order to receive such a precious booty. The hands from within too must go to work with there cycle of HIS time, to obtain a loot. And match it altogether to understand how, your purpose and clock is made. Here then, is your place, your life's destiny and rotation.

51

To Donzell 3/4/16 fri

Never forget the days of pain, so that you may remember to keep honor and give praise. Young man hold to your wits concerning this, and there will stay a smile on your face, like dew on a needed day. Keep in your heart WHO first took you to the dance, just in case there is know one around to tell you where to stand. For the leaves fall but the tree still remains. So is it for those that have HIS praise in there mind and HIS word in there hands.

52

Fill me with what I need always, not with what I only desire. when I need a glass of wine as a quick qench, when I need a glass of milk to make me feel good man that's a cinch. The taste of berry juice some how will hold me a while and will last. A full course meal may get me full and can be a blast. None of these tho compare to The Truth, The Way, The Life, or how HE fills you up with HIS filling FIRE.

53

Time as king and more than just for a day. How did it began? or keeps it stay? It was there before you and I, and even the milky way. before the sun, the moon and dinosaures as they were being erased. To understand it, the same as with hair. Misunderstood and called unfair. It has servided life and death and will no matter what you do or say. The seconds and moments are at it's mercy and even persaution. How does it go on? How is it sustained. Well time has told me I must release this, and go my way. But that wisdom has let me see that, time is FATHER, GOD. And that HE is it's maker. amen

54

The heart can be bought. The pain can be delayed. The eyes can see what they want to see. As many feet move through out the whole earth, the truth or a lie is told. But still, a wrong that's done, is a wrong that has made it in a mind of lose penetration.

55

Love is an invisible spirit with a strong body and big face. Of an everlasting quailty, unstoppable, penetrating, and older than the ages. Times and many names have seen it's grace. For as silence is ordered from some dark place. There it is again, saying here i am, a new ready if you are willing to co operate. Love is of true qualities, honesty, fairness, kindness, equal opertunity, a spirit of good measure as well as that of good faith. Love is filling, as any fruit and does not decay. Whether it is sampled quick or for many, many days. Even as love has been under attack at times, it seems to regroup, shine again and showup at the next starting gate. I will try to keep my notes fresh about love especially the line that is highlighted. Real love, Not to be faked nor imitated.

56

Just add water, eggs, milk; to flour and so much can created. Place any fruit to the side you may end up eating the plate. The same is for humans mainly a lady. Once she is finished being shaped, there is no end to her variaty when fully baked. Most like fruit, the tipical are grapes. Both are very tasty and sometimes easy to shape. But I have learned there down sides to this date. And there are two differences that I know of, and that is, as I estimate. Flour can make you exsplode, a woman can slap your face. But hold on to your ingrediates, so you can start all over again.

57

The liar too, has there own buisiness. They open shop for the
weak minded, the silly of heart, those that like there fancy
tickled. As the devil celebrities, they hunt for a victom in all
conditions. Like the fisherman who does it for living. But
there gain is your soul; there gain is your honor, even if there
is some pain or it get's bloody. They will not return to clean
up the mess and the waste that they have left behind. For like
the vampire, they drain the body completly dry. But if you
deny them there way, by stopping how they recycle and fly.
Life shall be easyer, because they will die.

58

The call was heard, because the call was made. A man is down we are all in this race. The rush was on, no time for any type of delay. Across the oceans, remove the sands. No moments for guessing, no time to even trap a fly in the hand. No stopping to refill thine belly or give any a repremand. Contrive your dreams lay them at bay. For when a man is down, there is no time to wait. For what is the hurry?, some fool happen to say. But as he followed the crowed a little ways. He saw that it was he that they were trying to rescue and save.

59

Roses are red, violets are blue. But they can be very hard to see if the view is blurry from a jaded stare or a degree of many untruths. So then it must be ok if the vision is washed with straight facts into reality as to clear the eyes of the uneven and glazy past, which at times haunts and may menipalate us all. But by removing the lies. The (real pictures) should last.

60

Her kisses like honey, her hugs a salvation. Her whispers in the night like a sweet, sweet rain. She looks into my eyes and erases the pain. I can't comprehend the feel of her skin, as the way of the seas softing the clay. As that of the birds taking wings to flight. Tho the storms may brew, I will still look her in the eyes to say, I want to be with you. Such is how I feel when she and I make our plight. For when we are together I can truly believe; believe in a life of sights and sound; Oh let me say. Let me say that even my lungs seem better when she is around. And so it is my hope right now that this will never stop. For two hands building a house is better than one.

61

He who lives by strenght each day, lives by hope. For an once of strenght is a ton of hope. It can take such little strength to push hope. The ant has no muscle mass, but yet moves many times it weight. The plants or trees starts out tender and fraile, pushes through pounds of rock or sand to sprout upward or out anyway. But strength is an unknown, without the birth of a thought. A life must presed a birth whether spirital or fisical. However they all are driven by an energy. An energy which is co habitor with love. Love is the smaller and inner wheel that is the cause and effect inwhich all the wheels move another day. Because love has strength and will live, always.

62

Smile, because life can be a bad joke, Smile if someone trys to say there is no hope, Smile, as you walk out into the blizzerd cold with no where to go. Just smile, because you can as an anger makes you want to loathe. Smile if life gives or it takes. Did you not know that smiling starts more things to grow. The one thing that can't be stopped nor taken away, is your smile, not now, or any day. No not even if someone makes you feel torn. Why should you stop smiling? since they did not put it their when you were born. So, (Remember-Smile-Remember); for your sake.

63

Just a little sound, a whisper to track the storm. A twinkle is ok to see the glare, so that I may find the way to my location and won't be wrong. The noise, I wish it away. But how then could I know to take comfort in the quiet moments. The still of the winter a time to reflect. However tho, life is not frozen and the two are not equal atleast not yet. No more than an open hand from the heart would keep the peace to end the strife when there is lack of comunication or respect. Balance has the understanding factors that must not be missed. Which keeps all of these pictures in check, moving, as well as clear.

64

Seek your dreams. Run up the stairs, to try new hopes where others won't dare. Reach the heavens remove the lead, the weights, even the funny stares. Break through the yokes by decision. Unmask those of deception. Unmask them I say, to free your hands and take flight. Do it, as if it where your last moment of time. Win the game; kick, scream, fight. Make your way from the canals of hell. For this is not new of you. You have done this before. Just remmember not to long ago, that it was tinny you, that fought to be free, from the birth canal.

65

I don't care about the gorilla, I can make him shake with just one glance. I have no fear of the beast of the field, a shake of my fist would make them lose there hard stare. Why I could be a matador if choose, no panic; for I wear the big pants. The king of the jungle, I will have him eating out of my hands. But nobody needs to know all of this but me and GOD, because true or not, a true brave man, stores his badge in his heart.

66

The sea of many, many hands from different nations. Connecting all at once at different times for the same dance. Dancing in the same pace without asking for a concert on some stage. Performing a goal to start and finsh a way. They all know that they are in place. They all know that there is no escape. So the dance must continue on. Let none there in that place, block the motion, let none block for unrightous debate. The dance must never cease. For it is not man's say.

One small flag exist that no person on earth wants to wave up high, is shame. It is well known however and is born at many locations, and made on any day. On any face it can be found, adopting all names. It's banner no one has love for and the weight of it's pride everyone wants to erase. The fire from it, waters of the monsoons can bearly quench or help one to ease the pains. Like a an ugly homemade tatoo it sticks around, mocking you as cloth to a jelly grape stain. Oh the sadness and debasement which may incabate, because it carrys a life sentence untill you want to file for your freedom and a true seperation. Tho the fruits of shame at times can be strong. It has lost many, many wars, by The POWER of JESUS, just one name.

68

Earth, Wind, Fire, you've heard of those three elements. Give me a moment, I will give you a better song. A song that you have been singing a long time, depending on how long you have been around. No matter anyhow. This songs tune has a long track record. Before there were people, these songs earned a praise. It's beat we know, Sand. It's words we know, Air. It's lyrics we know of, Water. But we have not bossed them around. Why they can crush us like ants. Working with them can be a beautiful thing. For; Air, Water, Sand, they have the power. And they give the demands. If there is a problem with this truth, just test any one of them. And it may be the last time you sing.

69

Take me to the finish line. For what games are there left to play, since the waters are dry and have no taste. There is no need to gleam at it anymore. Why wait? The pleasure of the sunrise, with the churping sounds, only leads to aggrivations. Let good thoughts return or make there way to a new destination. To a new place they should go, where someone can have appreciation. Plug the ears. Answers now fight the questions only to muddle all debates. Even the eyes will not twinkle, as to clear themselves of a bleeding false provocation. If the wheel has stopped to heal the end of the day. Then should I not stop this race? Run, for what I say? The test is not read in vain by an empty head. So close these chapters of every book, and please lock there gates.

70

Forever love, love always. Never put aside, never pushed away. Love always, yours now, your today. None to kill it, no one that can put it on delay. Does any know of it? Please tell me where it is or where it stays. Tell it my address. Please tell it my name. Tell it that I will love it back and that with me, it will be safe. I have a home, a nest for it. And the rent is already paid.

71

These mountains are to high to climb. These hearts are to hard to command. It might be much easer to swallow a glass of sand. Seeing is believing with an old hole in the head. Stuck and dule can share the same bed. As does more and need. I guess if something is broken, it could look that way. A comprimise, a quick fix is not the remedy, better to kill the mascarade. But when the eyes are open the dark should runway. Atleast then some will keep there honor, no matter what everyone else has to say. Even tho the rice and bean combine to make a soup. A fact still has a glow, when the light hits it's face.

72

Songs, so many of them, what a thrill. Of every kind and type. Some man made or by angels at during there retreats. They really did not start on earth, that's why it can't be killed. But Im sure glad that they began when they did. Just like GOD, why even HE likes a good beat. Just sing a song of praise to Him and you will see. Hit a note for HIM, for the best award. Like HIM we all like a song. And it can help our hearts weather the blues. Tho fast or slow, whether it is cold or hot. With or without the horn or the harp. Some short or long. Some have a message and heal pain, stop hurt or harm. A song is nice with plenty of cymbals. Still nice too, ha,ha; a love song that brings back good, good memorys.

73

I was loured to a place with no air. But was told there is life here. Just breath in anyhow and be aware. As I began, it seemed that there was little light there to go by and not enough to live. But then I grew from the light within. I later had to removed my ears, because the place was so hollow, I could bearly hear. I then remembered that all of the notes that I needed were in my skin. As I moved through this place, hosted by many test of fears. I could hardly move my feet but a few steps. Feeling as a boat would on the oceans with no sails. For a while I had to learn to dream and fly both day and night. Oh my sweet dreams, I must not let them be forgotten. Before I arrived here, I would have them often. Those wonderful dreams were so well. I can still see them from time to time, thru that tiny hole of this prison like shell.

74

Eyes, worth more than gold. They also vary and out way precious stones. There value is so high. Both can sway many hearts and have manipulated a lot of minds. There powerful colors are taken for granted. Yet, there presence many desire. Mirror, mirror, please do as I say and let me see what I should see. keep my request. For you are the oars to my ship. And yes you help to get me to my destiny. But I am still your skipper.

75

My ruby red, silver, gold; rainbow sheet. It goes with me anywhere that I need to be. At times transforming into my street. Guiding me always through dangers and harms, tenderly adjusting my feet. And none can hide it from me. I know that it's there for my path and what I need. A bow of a different demension, over my head as a fitting crown for a just king. For my HOLY GOD; KING placed it there. And no one has enough power, to over ride what HE has done or what HE says concerning me.

76

Don't let any one tell you not to go to the milkyway. Why listen to there decay?, they have very little vision. Go there and be of good cheer. Try not to focas on a mystical heart with bifocals, but can not see anyway. Why stay in that sand box? when all they may do is get mortar for just only your feet. Go, Once they have exsuasted there weak sceam. Keep your eyes bright on a dream. For who gets much from anything unless it is handeled and tossed like the boomerge.

77

Follow, follow me. Follow me for more than what you have asked for and you will see that there is no end to MY fruitful shores. Follow ME I keep my word, for at my tharf you will never, never starve. Follow me, you will have no more questions, for in me is every answer. Follow Me there is no pain. Because it was only a trick from our enemy, that lies every day. Follow ME, for you, I have a better place and it is your real home, and their you shall stay. Follow ME, for true love. I have a sustaining measure of it, from HE, WHO is up above. For in HIM is love, of where I AM from. HE and I can never die. So when you follow ME, true love and all else, you shall now and always have.

78

The tops of the heads may get grey hair and do very little to the brain. The tops of the trees at times receive a touch from many birds, as if they were a throne. The clouds can be the seats for the stars, but never a home. And the sands have no honor for man and do not care about the size of his feet or his glory. For they are one and the same. Of this mankind should study, and always know.

79

Plant for me the rose and lilly for life; cover me with daises. Give to me the sunflower, while I can enjoy them, with the spring rains. Then see how my heart beats everyday. Bath me in pure spring water. If it is ok? Lotion me with all of the oils of restorations. Keep me in fresh air, let it not blow away. Deep, deep green grasses to help me meditate. Let me look at the high mountains to justify my excapes. All these things are simple, and they are my easy REQUESTS, so let them be made.

80

A storm in the head may bring a strain. A storm in the heart can cause the pain. A storm on the way comes with the rain. For some, a storm in the soul will make hopeful intentions derailed or even put on a time delay. But the sun pushes away the dark, and burns up the flooded waters from the monsoon rains. As a kiss brings a glee on the face. Equal is a sign of peace by the release of the fisted hand. Should a storm of anger take it's stand?, with it's graved suit on that's tailor made. Then it is set, these matters are still the same, the light is coming and the path will be clear.

81

Suspisions and opinions are made of the same recipes. And they both are simple to cook. They both just need heat, and any lid dividing the steam from the smeal. Attimes to the untrained, they seem to look great. But as with a little this and that meals. The cook is usually amune to the stinch and does not get sick from the bloat of the body that hides the depressions on the face.

82

I do not know about the thaw after the freeze, nor about the chill in the heat. For to plead of my heart to be at ease, when she is near. To command my flesh to not weaken me when she appears. It would be simplier to stare at mountains and turn them all into precious jewlry. The mercy that I implure because of her entry, has removed the brass rods in my joints that made me be hard and stiffy. Return to me those days of course. But from this overpowering free horse I'm unsure if I want to unmount. And so there are two connections which will not unplug, Joy and stuck!, but pleasent it is, for she is there source.

83

They play all day, butterflies, they do. Without a care in this world. Who sees them struggle? None. Against the air they do travel. In motion right to left, up or down. Living as if being controled by a line of holy desire. And doing it much better than anyone on a thousand foot tite wire. No need to wonder of the time limit of there act. They keep many glaring to see just why they have no enemies to attack. Watch them make one forget the word old. They are like songs to the ears. A good story for the eyes to be told. Never stop butterflies, Thank GOD, keep the show going.

84

My face is a mirror of a million people, that was once dust of the sands from the planet earth. Sharing the cosmos since the moment of it's birth. We are family members made by the same FATHER. Cooked and measured by the HANDS, in which no one has stopped. If I made glass jars; could anyone tell me against there style, shape or model? No! I would make them as I please, and how I would want. So don't be mad should you see this face again, when you look up to catch the next falling star dust.

85

Don't make my wheels role as the others are made. Make my star glow different so no eye will roll away. My feet, they take a another path, not always straight, sometimes even lazy. Speaking the same tongue, no thanks, for who should know when Im jiving, ahh what the heck. Kiss me on the lips and then the neck. They don't need to know my heart. Some might rearrange the strings. Then I may lose it's tune and it's hum like the harp. Forget this blending. It looks as if we all have the same hair and style, for the same occasion. All Im trying to say is, no thanks copy cat. please just go your own way.

86

A place with so many trees, there is one just for me to rest under to take a seat. There are more stars than any man can count. There has to be one with my name on it. The seas have enough fish to feed everyone with at least two each. The beaches have enough sands to also hold every man on earth's feet. There are eyes to see what is needed to see. And it is good to have your own dreams. But there is only ONE LOVE that shall forever sustain me. I am glad that this truth, is also free.

87

A wall nor gate is no more a bother than a window pane. the view through them is clear, just the same. With one hand and my will, they must vanish, as my goals are raised. A bark of the dog only works on the feeble, the bite comes later. You can walk through the pain. Heal yourself, the persciption says. Remember that there was no one to show you how to study this simple education. After a cool drink, let the ice melt so another life can have a sip of water to be saved. Why point?, walk even farther. I'll bet that someone helped you on your way. Help someone else to learn the tricks in life, make a nice story, return the favor.

88

Toys, you play with them to fill an empty space of time. Who tells the truth that should be used to fill an empty space in the mind? Lies are toyed around with when truth is rare and voidness snecks you from behind. Let's compare! Lies and toys have a lot in common I've noticed. But only one brings fun. Anyone can perticipate, any age, any name. Mostly they are used when there is nothing good to say or to think. Both you can keep or walk away from. But only one you can return, to a store.

89

Just my picture. I paint it flying past the skys to touch the points of the stars. And then come back to the mass, my second home. I awaken to the singing from birds again, here on this planet earth. To a dish of the freshes seeds and herbs. A nice clean arrangement, made easy. As I walk on peace street. Which lead me to the edge of beaches where I can rest my feet. I must stop now, blow a kiss to the sweet air which helps me to feel so care free. Oh, but now the night is starting to come, so time to leave. I pass the moon on my way, a cloud covers it. Somehow, I think it just blinked at me. But thank The LORD these pleasures have not ended for me. Because now I will return to her, who shares my light and has my rib. I have been blessed with a painting given to me, just how HE wanted it to be. How was it done? Please don't ask right now. Let me just finish living and enjoying the fine painted mixtures, and the way that things are on my color T.V.

90

These shoulders were born to hold thee. Take my hands, they are made to catch thee. Take my words, they can heal thee. But keep them for tomorrow if need them. For as the cow eats the green grass, and makes white milk to fill the young belleys. I share a cycle of this life with you. You may not know where I come from, and I may not know where you are going. But sure as the rains makes snow. We share the same home under one sun. The heart does beat as a built in alarm clock with a purpose by a director as the salmon does at a crossing to spaun. The stones already have a job. That is why you have fluid flowing thru the heart. For what good is a pearl? If it remains under the dirt.

91

May love hide from her enemys, let her not be covered by deceit. Let her lift the life of the willing and absorb them like the sponge. Go to her, oh willing one, go! take her willing arms. For she is calling. Just listen to her screams. Loud is her alarms. She knows that she must go to someone. She knows that she has to rest. Her love has been hovering to long, so her place now is your chest. It is you she has chosen, move quick, before she is under arrest. Do not say foolishly, I can pay her bail. Take her, for she is waiting. Don't wait for her enemies to bruise her, and drag her by the tail. They will try to contain her, if your heart is stuck in one location. Give her a home! she's yours now, if you are wise and strong, and can give to her your place, where she is trying to belong.

The sun never stops shinning on my side of town. You say why, You may ask how. The answer is easy. I never asked it to go down. And did not have to. Because we both came from past the clouds. And we both are the same. You can't say that's not true. Why you really don't know me. Were you there in the beginning? I can prove it. For the sun is my witness. Ok! GOD made me, and GOD made the sun. You can't disprove me, because it was the sun that told me your eyes were close and that you were asleep in those beginning moments.

Can a picture be painted with just one color? Who does such? I must ponder. I raddle my brain of this thought. Why not? I say to my self. A picture of just one color. But this one thought will not leave my mind, this question that I have all of the time. Things aren't plural, I think to myself out loud. Unless it's a bag of potatoes or sugar, painted raw. But it's ok. So then maybe I should just paint things the way that I see them or just ignore. And then it hit me. Prisimes! But what would I do with the potatoe skins in my early drawings.

94

Keep my seat among the living. Keep that coat near by in case of a freeze. For it will stop the chivers and that seat will help me to be at ease. No one cares what you may want or what you might need. Lost in the facts are what others may precieve. A guess, a notion from to many nightmares and to many halfbaked dreams. Just remember the details. A house is built with facts. But only if you want it to be.

I don't like being sad. For who started it anyway? Who cares? I should say. Aslong as they can stay away from me to keep the drips of there poisons as far away as the seas. Because true happiness is not in there being. Try to figure them out. I say not! It would be much easyer to get stung by bumble bees. I am content with a smile, even if I got the honey while the bear was asleep.

96

One sip of tea, one glass of wine. But nothing on earth has taking more credits than the apple. And no one asks it how or why. An apple a day...., the forbidden fruit, the apple of an eye. It has even gotten the blame for when people tell so many lies. It seems to be the boss. Poor apple. Atleast I know the truth. That is why I stick with eating more raisins instead of eating applesauce.

97

How is the math the same but answers all wrong? The earth has been spinning since the start of the sun. Which came first, the moon or the birds? GOD KNOWS! Maybe it does not matter, so long as when it was my time, I also got the call.

98

By a pond where there is no storm. With the trees near to control the angle of how the wind blows. A nice place to take my saxophone horn, to forget life and all of it's systems and controls. A nice place, like being at home, on a summers day with all of the windows and doors pulled open. The waters so still; a glance at no hurt or harm. With the feel of eagels wings. The leaves trickle down as if to say to me. It is only us here today. As they go on to say, no need to worry as you see, we all have safe faces. So come closer, go ahead put your feet on our private beach. And stay as you will, rest a while, from all of the heat. For it is always ok by us whenever you come, to appreciate the moments and the times of being born and feeling free.

Living in the stomach began you. But now you start life, you do, the first moment out of the womb. Begin your hopes before they who gave you life make it to there tombs. Renew life any day as you grow to realize that you are getting older soon. Understanding that life has to keep moving. Be wise! Sustain all life, as your maturity starts to remain. Make life more pleasent as it starts to wain. Thank GOD ALMIGHTY for life and all that HE gave, before you are put into the grave. The ups and downs they've come and they've gone. But take JESUS with you, for beyond, TRUE LIFE and fun is now yours.

100

It rains always. So should not true love keep up? Since the start of the sun it has been raining to nurish the life made of the dirt. A HAND had a doing in this, to keep life's rotation and purpose. A design created from up above, made, for you and I even if we don't care or know it. Humans can't stop all the rains. And thank GOD they can't stop TRUE LOVE.

101

Pull, pull a train says. But it can't say i hurt. So when your load is to heavy. Let go! before the wheels come off and run you over.

102

A lesson I wished was always told. That is that tears sneak up to crack your face. They try to appear to end your flow of faith. Breath a while longer as to block those pains. Stay on your path, burn through the pace. Then lift your hands towards the heavens to notice your rainbows face. Which has always been standing their and waiting. Move forward, put a hand at each end and hold. By the touch of your hands reach and grab your hidden gold.

103

If I were the waters, I would clear the airs to shame the stink. In that moment stay around to give many a history lesson and a restoreing Drink. I would seek not fame nor furtune and arrive before any could think. My way would be a Refreshing salvation. My postion I would hold up to in HIS creation. I would not complain of the many jobs I have been assigned nor of the multiple locations. For I would be made to serve at HIS discretion. Because HE called my beginngs as one of HIS tools, to do HIS good biddings. I would not Cry, or do any snibbling. Appreciations, I would oftain Wave. My tasks would be uniuqe, at times in life and where Im needed. I might have to renew a balance, but my name concerns me. So while I can in my Flow, let me say that it's okay to be called water. But it looks like I should be called Equal. Because tho the dew brings a moist. Without me. How would the others live and behave?

104

Can I tell you of my philosophy? Someone Yelled. Tell me, I want too know of your thoughts. I then asked, but why don't you tell me of yours. Maybe your Words would be better being said to me. Hold me close, it was then said to me, don't you know we were meet to be. I'am Facts, wakeup, this is not another dream. At that time, I race in my mind to see the many words in my life of which I have been shown. But of the many replays, was all I heard, of the countless situations from my time here on earth. Not one would show of right or wrong. Just a jest here, or a, I think there. Some could not prove ethier if life was fair. But maybe the one thing I have learned is that the day comes whether your eyes are open or closed. Until a decision is made. That reality shall not come. Tho the shun of facts get blurred. No matter how you twist the words. Yet still, without proof, Philosophy is still untested, unstudied, lose words,

105

Is this fake? Is this real? How could I see so much a dream in my seeds? How could a reply come through my screen? I could not cast such a net of my own. A catch like that; I would have broken the reel. Such a situation had to come from up above. They mirror me, they go through me. And in my ears, they also say the same words. We all dance and play with each other like the clouds. Kids, Who is the adult? But the only shame is that, Im I just lost? No, I see, this is really normal. An older person reverting back in time as a tot. It's ok You see, cycles are good, and good comes from GOD.

Please ME, is what I heard, from a VOICE strong, but from a far. Past the galaxcies, light, times light, seven light years away. Who can I find, to sit at MY table? HIS voice had ecohoed. The eyes all opened to see what any would say. And then a cry was heard, hear one and all of HIS making. A tear was shed as the many could not stand. A glea was noted, a tremble preceded the broken bands. A PIERCING LIGHT then arrived with an unmeasured glow, ever calculated by man. HE is BEAUTIFUL, the crowds all said. As HE soon spoke, they knew that HE, was good enough to pass all that could always be ASKED or said.

What did the star say? It said that you are a fool with to much play, wasting time as tho life was some game. Figuring out rhymes as some sage, counting the numbers before you are payed. Promising love to a strange dame, seeing what is quoted but never flipping the pages. Take time my child, get a longer gaze. Study, learn, maximize your stay. There is only one of you my child, so there is no reason to lose your meditation. And should you decide to grow wiser, and live golden. Plant your eyes upward, remember your star, shine just as bold. This will help you to keep that mark, which is there as you change, in your life's time clock.

108

Stay with me awile, come with me among the moon and sun. Dream my breaths, take my belief. Give up lose free will, pay me with blood. Let us take together a vision as one and we shall fly like the doves. What I'am asking You is, let us marry to be one, with GOD blessing our love. You shall be mine and I shall be yours. As the fish and all other creatures in the seas. Let us blend and share life for a reason. Come with me now, but not in vain. Come before the wheel runs us over. Let us float together high on top of the waves, so that none can pull us down to the bottoms of the oceans floor. By man alone this is not possible, a perfect life, two true equals, becoming One. But in THE LORD, all things are possible, with all hands raised towards HIS throne. BUT wait! It only works by faith and decipline, and if You beleive that I'am Yours.

Taste, from the honey's of a life, that has sweet healing drips. Of which you are not familiar too. Just as some new place, in which has not ever been heard of or seen. Of these nice flavors one should adorne. Because of the untainted beginnings of it's fresh start. Dream at peace into it as you exspore. And inhale at will as you enjoy. Live now, for once. Is'ent this, what you've have been waiting for? Come now, open up, as you have never done before. Here you are, every path being grounded up by your feet, as the finest of some spice, pressed against the stones. With flowers all in bloom now. just where you knew that you should be as a worthy student. Keep in your heart that trust which you had always groomed. Don't doubt, or try to return back to those lawless street bruises. For the true life that you believed you should have, Today, it is truley of yours.

110

The fool with to many assesets of assumptions of tomorrow.
Can not reason on a fact which is an obvious. The outside or
the inside, are not these realities in opposite? The left, maybe
the right is an option. But they are of definate directions.
To miss cue good, then to make evil a prize, does not clear
the land for prosperaty and dreams for tomorrow. The man
meets the girl, not for the fog of just companionship, or to
help him load his borrow. Just as the wisdom of the eye sees
that the food looks good to help sustain life, for tomorrow.
Thus the unification by them as a player in a chain of purpose
and duty as platforms of foundations, singing in hormony
with the cycle of life, with a conclusion because there was
a start. An idle mind set will not move a force of truthful
answers nor ernest thought. Not even with the best of wishes.
But by light, with hope designed with truth, is guess work
on lazy thoughts put to death. If there is a desire to continue
life, as much as the heart may be content for that dream for
an everlasting tomorrow.

Fade to black. Chase a ghost. The answers within. For what is a dream? But why ask of it for only a penny. Is it not of better worth than dirt? Do not good hopes which are meant to do well, hold much more weight in the heart as the picture of the dream starts to a have glow. Make the statue without the wet to see if it may hold. But keep the glass of water nearby for the sip, for soon the thirst will be heard. For the water has not given up. Given up, on the many task of a creation. Should The Creator say, of a certain creation of to many stains. Why wash the garments? Is it not easier to just sew new raiments? For the new should bring YOU much praise. Consider the burn of them. Why not reliquish the pains. But a silence in a moment does not replace the love while in labor of that pressing desire when the total contents are of YOURS. The right of way is yours, if you are first.

112

Of this foggy ground. On this circle spinning around and around. Trying to hide from the junk and noises. How did I let this begin? Take hidden steps, take unmarked climbs. I queitly said! But another voice said to me. Remmember the dust comes from all directions and lands where ever it soposes. But wait! I said to the voice. Before you leave. What will be next? What else should I expect? And will you be there to assist me, if I should request? Just keep going forward is all I heard. As the voice repeated thru my void. As I carried on with my daily and life aspects. I began to see. Hey! maybe I need a new beginning. Then came a laugh of releaf. Like a sage on time, with daily wisedom. A storm passed over. But nothing happened. I was feeling blue with my head in the sands. As if grumpiness was a gift or a smarter plan. The junk and noise. Just did not want leave. But while waiting for the rains to clear. I noticed that the birds were singing a newer theme. It was tho they were making a different sound. Shame, was the tune. But of a personal rhyme. By then I took the time to look up at the passing clouds and notice that the noise in my head, had all but subsided. Then it appeared, as if I got a revelation. Hopefully it won't be forgotten this time of me, that fog may hide my destination. A note to myself aswell, that standing still with a long face will not solve a thing. And that if you let your inner lights grow dim, seeing won't be your only delima. It will be realizing that you are the only one who does't get it. And stuck is your gear.

The HOLY SPIRIT, taste of HIM. The sweetest of wines. Adore of HIM and be absorbed. The best of love. Meditate on HIM as you enjoy HIS WONDERFUL sounds and leading voice. Measured out from HIM, onto you, there will be no slugishness or void. A first kiss on HIM and will forget your first flights. Smooth as new skins will be your nights. Sing a song to HIM, and you will receive your rewards unfamiliar to you than those made of the dirt, from here on planet earth. Setting your eyes on HIM will return a joy. And make you not know of war. Do HIS (WILL) in do dilagence to live in gold. Of everything you my be told. Life on earth gets old, as some may know. But touch GOD and you shall have a different glowing story.

114

Who is it that may not hear a sound and yet understand more than us all? Those who are with GOD, I say. For there thoughts are unfettered, there veiw unchained. There rope to reach higher understanding is easliy untamed. For being now with GOD they have everything. There playground is large. There dreams have more exscape. Because GOD is great, so everything in HIM and around HIM must be the same. Oh what a day. What a moment, to be in HIS Great place.

Much are the number of trees on earth. Some are called jungels, woods or forest. Whatever the location or quantity. Feet travel in there mist or between there stomps. Feet of every shape and make. The trees don't consider who's feet enter there space. For trees were made to be strong and of an humble caring nature. It could even be possible that they are here to help teach even about sharing. I think this is so, because they help out any bird on delivery day. What a day, walking and looking at beautiful trees and giving thanks to (HE), WHO was kind enough to know that they needed to be made. But wait! One day while I was in my praise, my feet and my eyes were interrupted by another voice of thanks. It was a voice from within me saying, uh, uh, uh; i have to get in my thanks aswell, even just the same, as i pull in and push out, because of how they, the trees, help in clearing the air ways, to make for me another breathing day, like good solders do in a battle fray. So count the many tasks of trees, and you may just give up a praise that you did not know you had, or that were at your feet.

116

If I could, I would wash myself in mercy. For it pours easly and never burns, nor freezes. It removes tears and blots out decieses. It brings in a clean LOVE wheather or not it is needed. It knows me by name and calls me by it to feed me. It covers me boldly when my life stinks and flushes away any stupid pride to make it shrink. As I am standing licking the wounds of this mortal clay, mercy also jumps in to pertcipate. I can forward on now, because HE, MERCY, has again established my stay.

117

The blood thickens during the cold. As you grow older it thins in your veins and slows. What is the measure of it? Is it worth more than all of the gold? Someone thinks so. Who's blood you preciously swam in and stole. It is a quick answer. We all should know. Nine or Ten months seems to be forgotten by some. But NOT by most.

118

Quick kiss me on the lips, before I sobe. No wait three minutes until I can tell who you are. Don't blame me for not knowing who you are. Sorry! I was in a rush, and got fixed on the stars. Now let's try this all over again to see if pretending is a faurs. Oh, I see, it is just like lying. It will only last for a few moments while hot. So keep your kiss. For as the stars are of fire. Just the same. Your kisses really burn a lot.

119

Grow a new thought, see from the other side of the dark. Go, For they, the others won't know of it. Go, Lift up your style that is of you, a standard that has been burning in your heart. Go, For there desert of earth has stopped. For this is of you, a fresh and fruitful thought. This order can be raised. So make it spring up, you are the land that can produce a much better crop. Your grounds are new and ready. As the sun and rain have been waitng on your day, go in asurity as they do by the MASTERS PLAN. Take your set place. It has been okay for you, as you can relate. But you should know that no doors were open for you. You had to do that with your own two hands.

120

The heart sometimes paints pictures of different colors. But not painted are they always with a plan at the start. The finished product is slow or grudgedly. It has been learned that this earth was made with fire, ice and solid particles in time, as it turned. Was it a measure of a design even in the burn? Good things have (lasted) long because of the ingrediates in time. I have wrestled with a hope in life. But only because I did not see that it could not be a complete design, without all of the many colors which are in time. For who has ever defined colors? And why are they in the designs of time. So many colors are hidden away from the soul of the blind. As for me I hope to keep my mind (clear), so that I may see the many colors that time may provide.

Thunder and Lighting can be frighting, but so to is untested love, depending on who's doing the driving or who's going on the drive. The winds seem to command them both, before you can even blink an eye. Quick, can they both come and go. They both deserve respect. And of that, they both will remind you of so. There powers are wild. And sometimes hard To know. Just what they are going to do. Why it could be just easier to guess on every star. So then is it better to just duck and hide, when either passes by? Well I'm not the one who should answer that for anyone, at this point in time. Because, from now on, I will stand to the side and watch them both pass on by, to strike in the openess for the unsuspected who does know of their serious bite.

122

Question, How much is to much? Should you eat until you throw up? Is justice delayed, justice denied. What really floats your boat? Do we ever look on all sides? Can I be happy in love with the first one which comes my way? Is saddness a cousin to rain? Does what goes up always come down?, even tho no one understands how. Is another bite at the apple the result of greed or a head start on the fear of dying. And of course. Should I take my hat off before going in? or is it just easer to cut off my feet before I start? Well the answers are in the eye of he who beholds. And to the highest bidder, a new answer will be told.

My happiness in the storm. In the storm, in which I thought was so wrong. It looks so dark, it appears so strong. The spinning and twirling around, like grass blades across some road. The fires of the clouds. The noise that is made. I search for something to hold on to, but they all seem to exscape. As my plea for security often returns back to me with a fading period of delay. My tear ducts at times act as if they wanna go crazy. It's weird, I did not know that with so much time behide me now that I could return to being a baby. For like many others, I had heard that life is what you make it. Keep the book, don't worry about the worms eating the pages. Well, that could be true, but I was not told about the severe storms behaviors. Oh, but wait! A light is appearing and at it's sides are two doors and two gates. And at the end of the flood of hurt, is a glow with a spiraling stairway. Well I gotta go now, because the angels have been very patience. And with them, my head is out of the haze. Because my total happiness is in a new book, not in those short last papers.

124

Come home, shoot over the rains. Now is the time. The end of the navel has called it's day. Forfeit childs play, the many games have all now been tabolated. This place is a better palace for you, this place is your true station. No need to fight the separation, come on through. As many have done so, and have forgotten the pains. Dreams are no more, whispers in the night froze at the gate. Even here tears are not known, because here, trickery is not ordained. Joy is now your sphere, and your feet have become silver skates. True rest is also the bed inwhich no one can ever take away from you, or tell you that you can't have as a mate. So welcome love. The waiting is all over. Pleasures don't stop here, because time, is not in this game.

Is Skin just skin. Should you go farther to know what is beneth? Can you see the earth's core from the top of the trees? Harvest the crops, why consider if the ground has been diseased. Could it be that if we were god's we would all have the matters at hand and we would't keep trying to cheat. Open the door. Can't you control your sleep? The worms are in the mud as well, not just in the dirt which covers one's feet. But quick cover them. No don't, because you both are of the same hemisphere. Love has many wonderful legs. But you and must keep them moist and creamed. Does GOD see my thoughts, or is HE always to busy? To know of these matters however, is not that hard, nor far reaching. There is another way to weigh situations. But first you should go (skin deep).

126

Flavors of the clear or unseen. Of air, which was before man and is twins with breath. Of moisture, that makes no plans, and yet controls greed and wealth. Of life, as it begans as a thought then goes to a seed. Hope has it's start to create faith by using unknown jealousy. All circles turn at the command of a Will, WHO shares no glory. The desire to lead, must be done from within. For if done by the two incased with pupils the matter may get crossed and the victory for all is still undersedge. Which can halt a good life for many. For to have a family, you must first have a dream. So now the belly is very full of much to glean. Rest your head now on a fresh pillow of unvoided of pure beliefs.

Pass the clouds, my death doens't know of me. Can you, when it's time hear the row of the boat? The soft whisper going by. The noise of the train on the tracks. The extra cloths on my back. Note a quick question surprises the eyes. A wag of a tail. But you never asked how or why. The proof has not ever lied. And much is the confusions of life to keep many from a final answer as to stop them of excepting that portion of there pie. But notice the wet stream. Does not everyone drink from it? Is not there face also made of the same grit and grime? Is it not true that words of fact are much more even if they rhyme? Well looks may not be deceiving. And a man born here has no other exit ramp, or special bribe. For at his last and final bidding. There is no place anymore to hide.

128

It,(HE) flows on by if you get stiff or cold. The HOLY SPIRIT is WHO I am talking about, you should know. You see HE must keep moving; every moment, everyday, every hour. For HE is like a wheel that must keep on rolling. And HIS business is a lot of good works. No life in you, then HE will just keep going. Hold HIM, with a guess, a thought, a new birth. I know, I can confess. For many a time I froze up, on the ground and set on my hands like an unshelled pecan. It was like traveling around with a junk load on an endless road, but with no one to pay me for all that I've sown. So keep a spark of life within you to burn away any compounded debree of hurt. And then you may never have to worry about HIM leaving you behide, while being stuck on your island petistile. It can help to note some life events and mark each hope. As all your paydays in HIM, are still in what you treasure of your goals.

129

I study the sky, like watching fish go by. The way of man considering the scope of the land. Drift on thoughts, drift on. Keep a cycle to make what helps life's pregnecy produce it's fertile child. Nothing will continue on with a mentle block or being caught up in a rhut. Imaginery fields are sometimes needed to go in a location where one has never gone before. As a faith without a hope is dead. Can it be okay also to day dream for a while on a matter since so many keep on bumping there head. Who says that I can't wash my face with water longer to remove stubern cobbwebs. To take whatever time is needed is at the decretion of the beholder. And so then to receive a total knock out blow, sometimes one may have to pratice alone or a little more.

130

Go with me in to power. Go with me into electricity. The search is what is needed. Let's go into a womans true power source. She, the dust of the earth's undeclaried ruler. She it's life blood. For far so long she has beat her drum of notes with many a song, at the lost of her worth. The FATHER, gave to her a mantle and throne. In her appointed hour, there is no doupt that her significants is equal to any of HIS sons. Make propetual life without her. No, that is not of the True and LIVING ONE. If she is of just balance. Then no evil shall stand at any man's home. Her family will be rich indeed. And life on earth would be better for all of it's seeds. Try to poison water wells and drink of it. This is what life on earth is like if she does not know of her true purpose at the beginning. That is why she must be feed, from a rightuess table of knowledge and faith. Because her powers are not just for her. But ordained to bless what is of GODs. For her powers, given at birth. Are for healing.

131

A day of, or A day. A first walk. But who remembers but God and your mom. That first whistle, Can you recall. That first lie, Opps! was it a slip of the tung or some mistake. The happiess day of your life. Think, guess. Was it that first kiss in the school hall. Maybe it was when your heart drop on the floor and you finally came to GOD. Or was it your first bicycle ride and you let go of the handle bars to stretch out your two arms. Could it have been on your wedding day as you said to one another, i give you my all. Well tracking a history in a life is not unnoticed. As the forces of it will keep us growing or leave one in the end lonely. This is how life keeps a record of your heartful desisions, to capture it's truthful ways of each and every moment.

132

Can we together search to find the garden. On a path there is no question, when the desire is present of a certain direction. A time arises for a choice when one cares. Each, has a hunger positioned as a plan. Then let's us reach the top of a pyramid without any scandels. The goat eats grass alone. Does he instigate strife against the life of the nearby ravens? No! For they are conscious of there reality and enjoy the garden in which they share. But we are made in HIS image. How much of the lower creatures should we study before we reason. Watching the owl of the night is not where we were told to find our wisdom. So come, let us reach what was and is a good plan. But this time leave your burdens. For as fish do swimming easaly in the sea. Let's us to be pleased in our garden which grows everything we will forever need.

Only flesh Im I; of the earth. With a heart to pump the blood through out my body like the winds circlates the dirt. My stones give my skin a home as the joints hold them in one place. My feet given power to move by GOD and act like HIS thunder does for a time while on HIS creation. Oh what master pieces of divination. The brain made in my head, put there to lord over the whole body like a guardian angel. Even a cave is built in my throat. But not as an echo chamber. It was made to use words that help me, and to praise. As I think concerning my hands. They are not just ornaments. But are tools to work for GOD and a branch to help feed my face. With my eyes unblurred. How much nerve running through this member? Like the rivers yeild to the Great seas. What would it take to (see) clearly? I think, walk, breath, eat and exzist, because a GREAT source of POWER spoke, and made my spirit a sophisticated station.

134

Bridel your horse at the gate. For he doesn't know that he has plenty of races. Stroke his ego, time his paces. Let someone teach you how to rest his legs. For tho he is powerful. He is still your slave. This could be said of many things. As all things on earth made for man need deciple to balance them out for good use. And a measure of control or some time in the stable. Words are no less different. As wild words can hurt and kill, if left untamed.

135

Untie those strings that are not truly seen. Untie them, for they are not made of me. They were never known by me. A hold is not captivity, if one is awakened. Your knowlegde is within, so sneak free, break away. Seak not out the darkness as a victim. Tho it's arms try to trap you into it's systems. Of freedom, captivity does not care. For tho it knows that there is a Light, respect of it. It will not share. Fettered rage can be a spark light. If you think that Iam the one that will be a child of the night. The Savior, my Banner has shown how not to ever be a pawn in your cave. Thanks to HIM For freedom, Im I born for this campaign.

136

I reach towards the sky to touch those heights. For my place is there, from whence my breath had arrived. This location is not of mine. Because it has tears that has given a name to all the clowns. Take me up, deliver me back home. With lighting speed. Come take me back to that honeycomb. Let me depart. From the sleeping clamerise multitudes. For back at my true station, my wings can spread further. And it is there also, that my freedoms are unknown. But until I go and return. I must keep my head lifted up as a mark. Remind myself I must, that down is not greater than up. But as I leave the dirt for above. My feet, I can wash with there floods.

137

A story untold is as bad as a joke stuck in someone's throat.
Tell your story. For it may just give hope. Release it now.
Release it today. Your life's tail is as important as a train rails.
It is about where you have come from, and where you intend
to sail. Makeup now your life's notes. As this may be your
card or ticket, should some part of life attempt to arrest your
soul in some jail. There have been many who have forgotten
past events, good or bad, and wished later that there memory
did not fail. So a kiss under the moon is good. You could
have said to each other we will marry soon. You lied to your
parents, they hugged you, and forgave. And then you all went
to bed. But who kept all the notes, for all the days ahead?

138

Make a stand, tie a ribbon, wear that ring. Commitments are what life is truley about. They reflect what you believe. Set priorities are not made up Dramas. Rememmber that horses only show off to gain there first species of woman. Law and Order, hook or crook. Who you truly are, may be up for debate. And either of these, depending on which one you pick, may seal your faite. In life a many go the way of indecision. But only later to cast a wish in a chance of superstitions. With a finger in one ear and a pinch of the nose. For only if they could have learned before hand, that a seed must go into the ground, if you want something that grows.

139

I pawned my heart for a day at the beach, for a lonely daydream to see if it would speak. As my mind begin to ask, Why are we here? But the millions of thoughts kepted blocking my visions. As the many of waves seam to move with every heart beat. I released some of the pains with each bent of the neck, to see if it would help to keep up my stead. Oh! but no one cares, I said to the waves. And then they stopped to allow me to pray. Even so it also seemed, the sun did't burn as much, as I curply said, in my moment of savility. At the end of humility, the seagals began to land, with a loud, loud scream. As if to say. You can go on now, your prayers have been heard. Your prayers have been said.

140

The goats, have all gone. My sheeps to sheer, I have none. The stones and robes, why there is only an empty drum. The booty of my youth, when shall it return? As the times of Life may lean one down or forward. Wishing of a moment of sharing, as the many tests occures. In that time of need, is there a hand to grab hold of? Who can, if any, obsorb anothers storms. Or with care and understanding sheild them Of the blows? With every thought in mind. As much effert by a concerned person could find it's way at a dead end road. So at this turn It is true to say. All have lungs on earth. And the air we may trade. But no one can pump your blood. This is reality. And the brusies that I get in life, are my own, and possibly my own to face.

141

Tingly fettered beverages is the rain. Soft bottled whispers left in the sand. A coat of brusing wine hanging on the stands. Now where am i? Is what is repeatedly said. Can I return back thru that tunnel which began this maze? Should life on earth be replaced with blackouts of outerspace? A question comes and goes, while screaming a name. As foriegn then was the taste, of resilution in a bitter sweet matter of a day. It has forever been two roads. The contriversy is. Which of them will be clear to take?.

142

An angel kept screaming from the top of the heap. For a damsel in distress, another lost sheep. As she continued with her head dancing to the move of her feet. The messages of wisdom, would never cease. A dream in the naps shook her at ten. At twelve years old, they appeared through her parents. In one accord was there plea to her. Behave child, and learn to be managed. Before thirtyone while driving, two highway signs said on a low grade; slow down, brake. Afterwards, she told a friend. All can remember is the pain. At fifthty, a voice yelled out. You should be ashamed after all this time. But her reply under her breath, was. I don't need no guidess. Long before the age of eighty she started to talk with the angel. And he said to her. I m glad your now up here. As she now listened and asked him why. He answered her with a small frown. Because down their on earth, you about to drive me to lose, a very earned gown.

143

The sunflowers and moon, Weighed under the same scales. Neither two seek self fame. Some appreiciate the sunflower, as they highlight the lands to give them a name. Giving minds a thought to consider. A thought which is always the same. Wow! What a creation. The walls have art which were made by hands. Should you have been there as they where Raised? A question appears of equvalents at the middle of a night. Where did you come from? Is asked of the oval matter which glows by a great light. How did you get way up there? Can you fly? And Who brings you back to this location everytime? These created wonders tho simple to see, by curias eyes which should measure the fuctions of even the human body. Nails and hair, far to much as alikes to compare. Think! Has there distants stopped you from trying to use them as a prope, all for a praise.

144

Olive oil glitter glorious shines, are what I want of you in the mornings. A new cycle of life keeps the heart happy and young. The daylight breaks thru, now that bitterness is gone. Good things bring joy and are made to replenish. My hunger can be satisfied by the yield of your orchards. Does the winter lord over the spring? No, the world keeps on spinning. So then return to me oh joyous face as a new song. I will be looking for you, as soon as I awake.

145

The tone of HIS VOICE makes me soar. I saw HIS LIGHT and began to live. I dream of flowers but did not make them. With every glance at a tree that helps me praise thee. Your correction of fire is as lighting. The wisdom from YOU helps me rest. As does YOUR knowledge set my bones in place. All is real because of YOU. Honey is always honey because of YOU. Water is water because of YOU. Sweet dreams are sweet dreams because of YOU. Even when I increase, it is because that YOU have made the air so clean. Such quick kisses I never knew. Every day is reduced to a twinkling of an eye of joy because of YOU. As the water helps the iron smith. But it is only the sweet smell of duty at work. Like the knives before the attack. YOU sheilded me from the wounds. YOU are not like man. And I'm not YOU. Even tho many sought my blood. I did not fall, because they could not penetrate YOUR LOVE. So then be, and stay as YOU are to me, MAJESTIC,TRUE, BEAUTIFUL, and STRONG. Because YOU are my ALL and ALL.

146

The matrix is not void of many fruit with no dreams. It is empty of the death of many seeds. Apples, grapes, nuts, melons, olives trees. What may return the best yeild? I stood alone in the open wilderness awaiting for the meat that would satisfy a hunger from one of those trees, to then end up on a shore with a flowing breeze. But how can I be filled, I asked of myself, by a grove that smells like that it might be deceised? As the roars began to cease, I began to hear a voice which said in mine ear. Come, let me show you a fill, that you should keep. It was said to me, but you are the one that must receive the first green. As I streched out my hands towards the early morning sky. And then washed myself in truth all till the daylight. Until my tree had run the time. I have always had plenty of praise, faith, joy, strength and love, as long as I've stood in that soil, which had feed my roots throughout my bloodline.

147

A hard beverge is hard on a bottle. The full meal is much for the empty stomach. Sing your song next to a blue jay, the tune may lose it's bars. Vanish my hopes with the surprised temptation for a while; any hand can be stopped. As a sleep does all day, making no pleasure for the heart. Yet a thing is done. But was a mission well suited for completion.

148

Those lips, they move so much. Like leaves in the breeze, a wonder could be made as to who really controls the strings. Some minds are left to quest. Even pearls nor diamonds may effect such mared request. Dazzeling reactions, are what they've began. As eyes watching a ferris wheel, trying to keep up the pace. A goal I endeavored was to get them to cease, that I might hear again hear a sound of the moving sheets. Well, guess it will not be today, because after a long nights sleep. Here they come once more as the motor does, with enough grease.

149

Kids, playing in the rain. Don't they know that they're not ducks. What could they be thinking? I may have an answer. But, I can't remember everything. Is it ok when I sing to myself while making a day. You see; does anyone really change, even as they age? I have taking many chances throughout life and never ended wanting to ask the truth of any matter or joke and horseplay. To laugh or cry is a character. It hasn't removed my strengths. And love has no time limits and carries with it a universal name. Innocents often travels with love. They can be delivered sooner or later. Given of by GOD, that includes while even hidden by a navel. Kid's, maybe they have it all together after all. This may not be to hard to consider. Just look at the world, as it is run by us adults.

150

Eat from the tree of Life. When you are full and digest HIS commandments, you shall not die. Stay in that garden of balanced thought. For if you are inticed to leave you will only be lost. Of HIS wine is good health. A press was made that HIS issue would be dranken. And it is good to eat and drink of HIM, that life might be sustained. And that death should not know of your name. For who enters a desert looking for life and laughter? Only the foolish do so, to fill there voids of any desire or matter. Seek not the vain supply. But go to the tree, of Everlasting Life.

151

Animals can't be dumb. Who taught them what they know; like how to hunt? Who is the game? Need I go to a hill at contemplation and notice if the life of man is as welly organize as that of the ants, to admit which is truley lame? Did animals learn from you of the ways to build there nest's? Smarter are they than humans also when it's time to rest. I don't swallow water, as they do without my heart beating like three drums, out of my chest. I inquire of myself. Was and is, it really that easy to listen to what GOD is saying?

152

Traces of lying minds, wondering what they can figure out, looking for the driest places. They will not give away any find. Fish don't live by a clock, or jump up to the ground. Because it is not there home. And they will not seek out the bee for honey or get jelous of the height of it's hive. A mother, does not hold her hand out of repayment, as soon as the child arrives. In the place which holds drought, will be found a lie. No solutions exits there, so the only cycles are another dry place, into another lying mind.

153

As rays on the back in the morning, and like light on the face at noon. If a night should fall. I must remember that location. Tho even with the cold, it is still okay. Away may seem to win the day, but HIS beam finds me when I stray. Maybe if I stumble in a step or lose that measured true calculation. It shall be orderd for me to return again at that essence of purest energy, which is my salvation.

154

Shame me no more, oh fair lady. For I have brought gifts of words to help ease those pains. This will be, as the corn has to grow and the rose has to bloom. The night is still ours, so let's exsape soon. Please be at rest, do not create a shame. Open your paths, for me that i might show my raise. I have more to give. You have not seen my best. Surprises and hopes, shall all say yes. Of you within, is a goal like a high nest. And it is a bounty, which i have claimed. Who could have said that death is known to yes? Look no more away from me, even the brick surrenders to clay. As age is to grapes. The union shall be great. So let it now be fulfilled in a peace, as the earth does spinning, in heavens space.

Double your bet on your way up to heaven. No more crimes, no more mind games that might set you off. The road is clearer now with HIS word, because you are at the right doorstep. Time to get it right. Yes! that's what HE said. The flow will be easy. The smoke from the hurt won't be needed, to keep you in check. Few have done this, but of you is the next step. A decision has been made, if you want richies and rest. I like an easy path. For the road before was only of the very hard headed. Choose a path today. I'm glad that I heard those words through the smoke. As I can see now, there is no comparision.

156

What's happening here, on earth while GOD is waiting? What's HE doing in time and or space? The earth spins without your approval. And it has not waited for man's ok. I don't need to worry about what GOD is doing. All I need to keep doing is listen to what HE says. Can you hear the whispers? Can you understand the words on that face? Hunger for the message, seek out the pure language. Set is the process of living from day to day. All other questions have wasted what should be a very pleasant situation.

157

Eyes which pierce thru and across the galaxies of dark and stars. They never sleep as you or I are. They see thru the clouds, they see thru every heart. A mystical order commands their charge. Their way is to watch and observe the conducts on planet earth. It is a job which intells much concern. As they record and reflect a life, even before flesh life at birth. The depths nor graves, won't block their view. And no matter if you attempt to hide, those Eyes will find you. For always on duty are those Eyes that can pierce thru. Because such are those Eyes which were before me and you. At all fronts, and on all sides, every morsal or grain are found. By the Eyes of indefinite knowledge. Even the winds don't get lost. So bid not their vision with one sceam. And a readjustment by eye fluids are no good for The Eyes, which never had lids.

158

My heart is not a sailboat. It should't swim from shore to shore. Blood and concern, an ocean which if misdirected can cause more pain than a hurricane storm. Tho they both live by warmth and choice. Because many don't care that their actions are a loaded gun. Cause and effect, has left many to mourn. I don't care, some think, especially if i'm ok. But who pays? Well study the waters and you will see all of the spilled blood that stinks, on the shores.

159

Fast, fast, was I going. It was like a panther was chasing me on a waxed floor. To and fro, sidewades and long, without stopping until all of my strenght was gone. The bite of a fruit. The signs were their. But I needed someone to tell me to free from that maze. But! run, run ; my thoughts said to me, while in the heat or while under my own songs. Life, has a way out. Or a cheating sheet. Don't wast time for proof. You will eat of everything soon, were the words that I fested within by my narrow schooling. And since you are you're very fast. Your speed or height of the trees might save you. But as I drugged my tested love to what I thought was it's final resting place, it came to life again, to put a bite instead on my dugler vein.

160

Her tear fell on the ground today, but her faith was picked up. Down the slide, shoes with a smile, no questions why, just go for the ride. Down the street on a rainy day to work in a gleen, no mind of wet feet. Her story may arrive in a scream, but so long as it finishes on an even heel. Many of the parts may not be in life always. What matters is that she tries to make a good mark till the end, so that everyone will remember atleast she was a true believer.

161

I stepped off into outer space. Crystal clear, oh what an understatement. My first glance at the passing sun, earth and moon, the spinning made me guit hazy. As I continued on tru the milkyway system. A song came to mind. Man, You have left everything behind. Wow, now what do I see? The stars and the whole solar system. With my soul at awe. A thought appears, but where is GOD. HE has to be near. I say to myself. Because my heart is racing and thumping almost out of it's shell. I call to HIM in a repeated pace. And still keep in mind that Im glad HE's slow to anger. For have I asked of so much from HIM? Life, liberty and the sharing of HIS creations. I pause again to think, of course HE gives to those whom HE loves. And youre surley in HIS love. How else, I say to myself, could you rise to even the heavens above. As I go now to my final destination. Within me poetry appears. As tho this all began in one glove. Well I should not end with goodbye. Because you never know who you might see, on HIS wonderful Kingdom ride.

162

What is a paradise? An embedded hope calls your name. Different places, different faces. On first arrival, things seam just great. But then comes mars, with it's dreaded grades. Will it do pushing forward with a dream from the edge of the circle, to beneth the sands of the sea. Pour for me the making of every wine. Caress my lips for gifted reminders. Walk with me at sunrise. Tell me that each day is mine. Make my dreams as tasty as young spring waters. Order for me a place on any boader. Assumption! what a cold friend. A mascerade or faith. To think twice on a matter of which has not yet been studied by you is the forbidden treasure to find. On a trip to a paradise are some fires and some rains. No blurred decision may stop you, because the final result is your destiny.

163

The Blade of grass set counsel with a life inside of a belly. For the life had to much to consider, in the time of days. To many wayward thoughts had the life spinning. Sit with me for spell, as the blade said to the life, made from the belly. As the blade continued on with words in spades. Life as i know has been great, for i learned early on that you must give and take. Sunny days and nurishments, are not all that are allowed by The Maker. Strong winds and many steps may hit you in some ugly places. Lonlelyness may even come with a smile on it's face. Promises broken, promises kept, will leave one stagering in this land of inepte. But hold to on those roots which were given to you as markers or guided stripes.

164

They knew one day that love would plead to sit at there tables. Love is a treasure. But it is not the end should it have no where yet to stay. Picked is it, by the hands which can see a good thing. Hidden at times is it from wolves that may ruen it's name. Love; not a game, or a silly frase. So prepare your table for it, love. What a meal. But to eat of it. You must entice it, from it's secret place.

165

Truth is a good blow; not a ruff stone. Has your mind thought of such? It's hit won't hurt. Hunger for it. Should I not sit near it's throne? Hunt it like the foul looking for the tender meal while it's gaurdians are gone. Be as the prey searching the grounds from nest to nest, with extended claws, Going high and low. Show an egerness to be filled by it again and then some more. The one fact about truth is. It never wants to run.

166

Girls got questions also, this and that. Seems as if some don't, by the way that they twist there necks. Right or left there ponderment may have you guessing. The world is there apple, yes the whole alphebet. Not difficult is there heartbeat of a favorite blooming decision. For she's a revolving pyramid. Whistle in the wind! No! that's only of a man. For a man can get stuck at the drop of a hat. For a girl, one hunderd percent of whatever is there request. The question allums however. Why are they like that? Tho such a question deserves an answer. It won't be by me, because I'm not willing to stick out my neck.

Let us be near, as the birds are to the tree leaves. Let us want in harmony like the bee for the honey. Oh how I know that two equals one. But to start this passage we must share and learn the same love. Open my heart as meat to eat. And you will have it on a silver sheet. As it is known true worth is not cheap. Till my soil, Dig deeper. Then you may see a rest which replaces any missing rib. Come forth to me. For my hammer is not to bruise. Stake your quest with me, and there shall be no end to good.

168

Behold, a golden man, with pure hands. His wings soar far above the sands. He is captive nor discovered by no man. His story lasted my lifetime. His remedy has been my cure. I opened His door and forever budded even the more. My feet enjoy His emerald floor. In His home a multitude of faces stare at His High throne. As they know that non can compare, to His levels. Because many others, have fallen very short, of glory.

Printed in the United States
By Bookmasters